vince guaraldi

Arranged by Brent Edstrom

contents

Photo by Michael Ochs Archives / Stringer / Getty Images

ISBN 978-1-70516-868-4

Visit Hal Leonard Online at
www.halleonard.com

World headquarters, contact:
Hal Leonard
7777 West Bluemound Road
Milwaukee, WI 53213
Email: info@halleonard.com

In Europe, contact:
Hal Leonard Europe Limited
1 Red Place
London, W1K 6PL
Email: info@halleonardeurope.com

In Australia, contact:
Hal Leonard Australia Pty. Ltd.
4 Lentara Court
Cheltenham, Victoria, 3192 Australia
Email: info@halleonard.com.au

BLUES FOR PEANUTS

By VINCE GUARALDI

CALLING DR. FUNK

By VINCE GUARALDI

To Coda

A DAY IN THE LIFE OF A FOOL
(Manhã De Carnaval)

By LUIZ BONFA

CAST YOUR FATE TO THE WIND

By VINCE GUARALDI

CHARLIE BROWN THEME

By VINCE GUARALDI

CHARLIE'S BLUES

By VINCE GUARALDI

CHRISTMAS IS COMING

from A CHARLIE BROWN CHRISTMAS

By VINCE GUARALDI

Straight 8ths

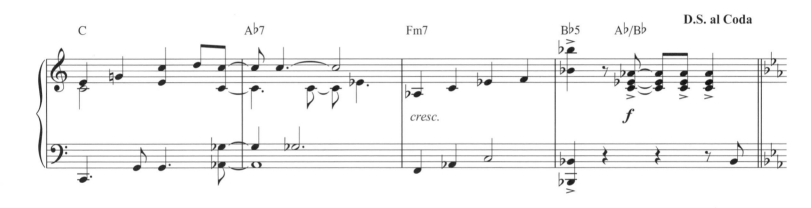

D.S. al Coda

CODA

DJANGO

By JOHN LEWIS

GINZA SAMBA

By VINCE GUARALDI

EL MATADOR

By VINCE GUARALDI

FENWYCK'S FARFEL

By VINCE GUARALDI

THE GREAT PUMPKIN WALTZ

By VINCE GUARALDI

CODA

HAPPINESS THEME

By VINCE GUARALDI

LINUS AND LUCY
from A CHARLIE BROWN CHRISTMAS

By VINCE GUARALDI

Straight 8ths

O TANNENBAUM

from A CHARLIE BROWN CHRISTMAS

TRADITIONAL
Arranged by VINCE GUARALDI

LITTLE BIRDIE

By VINCE GUARALDI

MR. LUCKY

By HENRY MANCINI

OH, GOOD GRIEF

By VINCE GUARALDI

Laid-back Swing

SAMBA DE ORFEU

Words by ANTONIO MARIA
Music by LUIZ BONFA

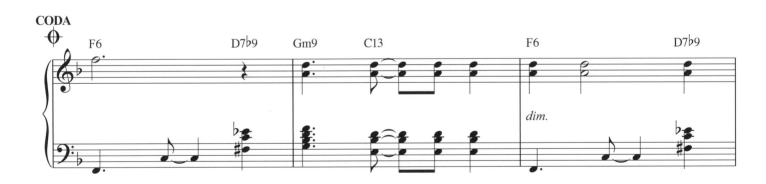

OUTRA VEZ

Words and Music by
ANTONIO CARLOS JOBIM

Moderate Bossa Nova

THE PEBBLE BEACH THEME

By VINCE GUARALDI

Moderately, with a Latin feel

To Coda ⊕

SKATING
from A CHARLIE BROWN CHRISTMAS

By VINCE GUARALDI

Bright Jazz Waltz

STAR SONG

By VINCE GUARALDI

TREAT STREET

By VINCE GUARALDI

The Best-Selling Jazz Book of All Time Is Now Legal!

The Real Books are the most popular jazz books of all time. Since the 1970s, musicians have trusted these volumes to get them through every gig, night after night. The problem is that the books were illegally produced and distributed, without any regard to copyright law, or royalties paid to the composers who created these musical masterpieces.

Hal Leonard is very proud to present the first legitimate and legal editions of these books ever produced. You won't even notice the difference, other than all the notorious errors being fixed: the covers and typeface look the same, the song lists are nearly identical, and the price for our edition is even cheaper than the originals!

Every conscientious musician will appreciate that these books are now produced accurately and ethically, benefitting the songwriters that we owe for some of the greatest tunes of all time!

VOLUME 1
00240221	C Edition	$49.99
00240224	B♭ Edition	$49.99
00240225	E♭ Edition	$49.99
00240226	Bass Clef Edition	$49.99
00286389	F Edition	$39.99
00240292	C Edition 6 x 9	$39.99
00240339	B♭ Edition 6 x 9	$44.99
00147792	Bass Clef Edition 6 x 9	$39.99
00200984	Online Backing Tracks: Selections	$45.00
00110604	Book/USB Flash Drive Backing Tracks Pack	$85.00
00110599	USB Flash Drive Only	$50.00

VOLUME 2
00240222	C Edition	$49.99
00240227	B♭ Edition	$49.99
00240228	E♭ Edition	$49.99
00240229	Bass Clef Edition	$49.99
00240293	C Edition 6 x 9	$39.99
00125900	B♭ Edition 6 x 9	$39.99
00125900	The Real Book – Mini Edition	$39.99
00204126	Backing Tracks on USB Flash Drive	$55.00
00204131	C Edition – USB Flash Drive Pack	$85.00

VOLUME 3
00240233	C Edition	$49.99
00240284	B♭ Edition	$49.99
00240285	E♭ Edition	$49.99
00240286	Bass Clef Edition	$49.99
00240338	C Edition 6 x 9	$39.99

VOLUME 4
00240296	C Edition	$49.99
00103348	B♭ Edition	$49.99
00103349	E♭ Edition	$49.99
00103350	Bass Clef Edition	$49.99

VOLUME 5
00240349	C Edition	$49.99
00175278	B♭ Edition	$49.99
00175279	E♭ Edition	$49.99

VOLUME 6
00240534	C Edition	$49.99
00223637	E♭ Edition	$49.99

Also available:
00154230	The Real Bebop Book C Edition	$34.99
00295069	The Real Bebop Book E♭ Edition	$34.99
00295068	The Real Bebop Book B♭ Edition	$34.99
00240264	The Real Blues Book	$39.99
00310910	The Real Bluegrass Book	$39.99
00240223	The Real Broadway Book	$39.99
00240440	The Trane Book	$25.00
00125426	The Real Country Book	$45.00
00269721	The Real Miles Davis Book C Edition	$29.99
00269723	The Real Miles Davis Book B♭ Edition	$29.99
00240355	The Real Dixieland Book C Edition	$39.99
00294853	The Real Dixieland Book E♭ Edition	$39.99
00122335	The Real Dixieland Book B♭ Edition	$39.99
00240235	The Duke Ellington Real Book	$29.99
00240268	The Real Jazz Solos Book	$44.99
00240348	The Real Latin Book C Edition	$39.99
00127107	The Real Latin Book B♭ Edition	$39.99
00120809	The Pat Metheny Real Book C Edition	$34.99
00252119	The Pat Metheny Real Book B♭ Edition	$29.99
00240358	The Charlie Parker Real Book C Edition	$25.00
00275997	The Charlie Parker Real Book E♭ Edition	$25.00
00118324	The Real Pop Book C Edition – Vol. 1	$45.00
00295066	The Real Pop Book B♭ Edition – Vol. 1	$39.99
00286451	The Real Pop Book C Edition – Vol. 2	$45.00
00240331	The Bud Powell Real Book	$25.00
00240437	The Real R&B Book C Edition	$45.00
00276590	The Real R&B Book B♭ Edition	$45.00
00240313	The Real Rock Book	$39.99
00240323	The Real Rock Book – Vol. 2	$39.99
00240359	The Real Tab Book	$39.99
00240317	The Real Worship Book	$35.00

THE REAL CHRISTMAS BOOK
00240306	C Edition	$39.99
00240345	B♭ Edition	$35.00
00240346	E♭ Edition	$35.00
00240347	Bass Clef Edition	$35.00

THE REAL VOCAL BOOK
00240230	Volume 1 High Voice	$40.00
00240307	Volume 1 Low Voice	$40.00
00240231	Volume 2 High Voice	$39.99
00240308	Volume 2 Low Voice	$39.99
00240391	Volume 3 High Voice	$39.99
00240392	Volume 3 Low Voice	$39.99
00118318	Volume 4 High Voice	$39.99
00118319	Volume 4 Low Voice	$39.99

Complete song lists online at www.halleonard.com

Prices, content, and availability subject to change without notice.